# Life in Tu

GW01454925

**CAMBRIDGE**
UNIVERSITY PRESS

# The world of the Tudors

Over five hundred years ago a very powerful family called the Tudors ruled England, Wales and Ireland. From 1485 until 1603 all the kings and queens came from this family.

There were many different kinds of people living in Tudor times: kings and queens, merchants and craftspeople, farmers and labourers, people who lived in the countryside and those who lived in the growing towns and cities such as London. Their lives were very different from ours. We can learn how people used to live from pictures, writings, buildings and objects. Historians call these sources. Sources give us clues about how people used to live in Tudor times.

At the bottom of these pages you can see a picture source. It shows how London looked in Tudor times. What can you tell from the picture? A picture like this shows what the Tudor world looked like. It tells us very little about people's feelings. As you read this book try to understand the thoughts and feelings of people in Tudor times.

What things are really important to you? It could be your family, money, religion, food or your home. In this book you will learn about the lives of different kinds of Tudor people. You will find out how they lived and what they cared about. By the end of your study of Tudor times you will be able to answer this question:

## What was important to Tudor people?

## Things to find

- How many of the things below can you find in the picture:

  the Tower of London
  churches
  ships and boats
  carts and carriages
  the countryside
  animals
  heads on poles
  people

- What else can you find?

# A Tudor city

London was very important in Tudor times. Merchants and traders made a lot of money in London. Without their taxes the king or queen could not govern the country. London was growing and many different types of people lived and worked there.

## What was life like for people in Tudor London?

> I am a rich merchant. I send ships to every port in Europe. I am planning to trade with countries as far away as India. I hope to be even wealthier than my father.

## Think about

- Look at what these people say. Why do you think so many people wanted to live and work in London?

4

I buy and sell woollen cloth. Much of it is sold abroad. I put seals on the cloth to show its quality.
I am an apprentice. My master is teaching me to make saucers and spoons. Many of them are sold abroad.
I am a widow living in a village outside London. I bring eggs and butter to sell at a market in London.
People pay me to row them across the river. More and more boats are carrying goods on the river these days.
I live in an alley by the riverside. Sometimes I can get work as a porter. When I cannot work I go hungry.

# A changing city

London was by far the biggest city in Tudor England and it was growing fast. Many changes were taking place. We can use maps and writings from Tudor times to give us clues about how London was changing.

▼ This map of London was drawn in 1572

## Things to find

- Find the city walls. You can follow them all the way around.

- Look for all the places where buildings are spreading beyond the city walls.

We cannot be sure exactly how many people lived in London in Tudor times. In 1500 there were probably about 70,000 people. A century later, in 1600, there were over 200,000 people living in London.

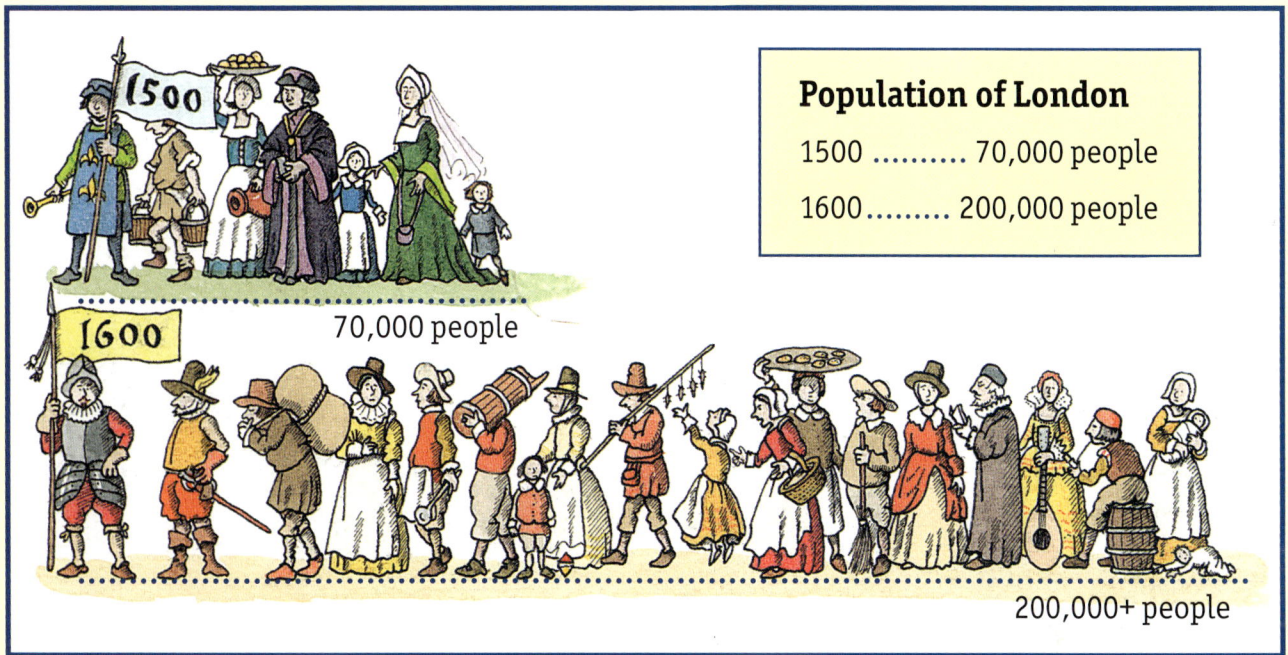

**Population of London**

1500 .......... 70,000 people

1600 ......... 200,000 people

70,000 people

200,000+ people

This diagram shows how the population of London was changing in the sixteenth century.

- The population of London grew much larger between 1500 and 1600. How many more people were living in London by the end of this period?

The main reason why London was growing so fast was that people were moving to the city from other places. The largest numbers of people were coming from Holland, France, Italy, Spain and Scotland but they were coming from other parts of England too. Many of these people brought new skills and trades such as glass-making, pottery and watch-making.

### Things to do

- Look again at the different Tudor people on pages 4 and 5. Choose two of these people. How might they have become richer as London grew?

A man called John Stow wrote about London in 1603. He described how London was changing.

## Traffic problems

The city council had rules which said that heavy carts were not allowed in the centre of London. They also said that carriages must go at walking speed.

*The number of carts and coaches, more than there have been in the past, is dangerous. By the laws of this city, the horses of every carriage should be led by the hand, but these sensible rules are not obeyed. The world runs on wheels, whereas our parents were glad to go on foot.*

- What clues does John Stow give us about how London changed in Tudor times?

## Too many houses

John Stow also wrote about the houses that people were building on the common fields, where animals were kept. People were not supposed to build houses there.

● Look again at the map on page 6 and try to find places where this was happening.

*Both sides of the street are crowded with cottages and alleys, even into the common field, all of which ought to lie open and free. But this common field, being once the beauty of the city, has many filthy cottages on it. In some places the road is not wide enough for the carriages to pass.*

● Why do you think John Stow was worried about the growth of London?

### Things to do

● Make a list of the ways in which London was changing. Use all the sources and information in this chapter.

9

# Country living

In Tudor times most people lived and worked in the country. They lived in small villages and worked either in the fields, in workshops or in their own houses.

## What was life like in the countryside?

▲ Husbandmen were farmers, but they did not own land – they rented it from wealthy landowners.

▲ Labourers worked on the land and looked after animals. Poor people went hungry if the harvest was bad. In very bad years some people in remote areas starved to death.

▲ Yeomen owned land, lived in big houses and had many people working for them.

● Which of the people in the picture do you think was the poorest and which was the richest?

▲ This is a picture of a harvest made in Tudor times. Look at the people on page 10. Which types of people can you see in this picture?

Well-off yeomen often built fine houses for themselves in the Tudor period. The poorest labourers lived in tiny cottages so flimsy that they have not survived to the present day.

● Which of the three types of people might have lived in a farmhouse like this one in Oxfordshire?

## Things to do

● Draw a picture of two different country people. Draw a speech bubble for each of them and write what you think they hoped for to improve their lives.

# The mansions of the rich

Rich and important Tudor people who lived in London also wanted a mansion in the countryside. Sir John Thynne was a very rich and powerful nobleman. In 1554 he ordered work to begin on his new mansion in Wiltshire, called Longleat. It was built with entertaining in mind, with large halls and long galleries. In 1575 Queen Elizabeth I stayed here while she was on one of her journeys around the country.

▼ This painting of Longleat can tell us about the kinds of things rich Tudor people liked to see in the design of their houses.

## Things to find

- Find clues that tell us:

  Tudors liked symmetry

  open fires were used to heat Tudor mansions

  this was a good place to entertain guests

- Find other clues in the painting which tell us about the places where very rich Tudor people liked to live.

Merchants and gentlemen also built new and comfortable manor houses.

▲ In 1515 Sir William Compton decided to build this house. He had a very important position as a courtier to King Henry VIII. This meant that he spent a lot of time in Henry VIII's household, serving the king as his friend and helper. When his house was built, it was by far the largest house in the neighbourhood.

## Things to do

- What clues are there that the owners of Tudor mansions wanted to show people how rich they were?

- Rich Tudor people sometimes had their houses built in the shape of the letters H or E. Why do you think they did this?

- Use the features you have read about to design your own mansion in a Tudor style. Make it as impressive as you can.

## Things to find

- Find these features of Sir William Compton's house:

  the large entrance

  the battlements on some of the towers

  the number of chimneys

# Inside the houses of the wealthy

One way to find out about the inside of rich Tudor houses is to read a list of the things people owned when they died. This is called an inventory.

This is part of an inventory of Sir John Petre's possessions. It was made in 1600. It lists the furniture found in one of his bedrooms.

Tapestry hangings, decorated with the story of Moses

A carved bedstead layde with crimson silk and fringed with gold lace

A little low table standing upon a frame, being walnut

A fire shovel

A pair of bellows

A high chair of walnut with arms, the back and seat covered in crimson velvet

A carved cupboard of walnut

- How can you tell from this inventory that Sir John Petre was a rich man?

This photograph shows a room in Oxburgh Hall in Norfolk. As in most Tudor mansions, the room is large and rather bare. Even rich noblemen did not own much furniture in Tudor times. The walls were sometimes panelled in wood and large tapestries were hung on the walls to stop draughts.

## Things to do

- Look again at the inventory on page 14. Make your own inventory of the furniture in this room in Oxburgh Hall.

- Now make an inventory of the furniture and belongings in your bedroom at home. Compare the two. What are the main differences?

# Kings and queens

We call kings and queens monarchs. When a country is ruled by a monarch we say that it has a monarchy. In Tudor times the monarch had a lot more power than a king or queen has today.

## How powerful were the kings and queens of Tudor times?

In Tudor times coins showed the head of the monarch, just as they do today. The coins in this 'family tree' show the heads of the five kings and queens we call the Tudors. The dates under each monarch's name show how long they reigned.

### Think about

- How do you think most Tudor people knew what their king or queen looked like?

- Which monarchs were Henry VIII's children?

- Which monarch had the longest reign and which had the shortest?

### *Edward VI* ▶

**1547–53**

Henry's only son, Edward, was only nine when he became king. The country was ruled by powerful noblemen because the king was so young. Edward was never very healthy and strong.

- How old was he when he died?

## Henry VII ▶

**1485–1509**

Henry VII was the first Tudor king. He took the crown after the Battle of Bosworth Field in which Richard III was killed. He was very careful with money. He helped to make the country strong and rich after it had passed through difficult times.

## Henry VIII ▶

**1509–47**

Henry VIII had six wives. This is what people usually remember about him but he was also the first king to take control of the Church. He spent huge sums of money on foreign wars and on entertainment.

## Mary I ▶

**1553–8**

Mary was Henry VIII's eldest daughter. She was not a popular queen. In 1554 she married a Spaniard, Prince Philip, who became King Philip II of Spain. Many English people feared that England would come under Spanish rule. Mary longed to have a child, but she died childless in 1558.

## Elizabeth I ▶

**1558–1603**

Elizabeth I became queen after the death of her half-sister Mary. During her long reign Elizabeth faced many problems but managed to stay in control. She did not marry and she had no children. She was the last member of the Tudor family to rule England.

# Courtiers and parliament

Many rich noblemen came to the king or queen's court. These people were called courtiers. They hoped that the monarch would notice them and perhaps give them a job as an adviser.

Elizabeth was only 25 when she became queen. She knew that she had enemies in England and abroad. Like all Tudor monarchs she was afraid that people might plot to rebel against her. Kings and queens had to choose their advisers very carefully, to make sure that they would be loyal.

The king or queen could only make big changes in the country by making laws. However, monarchs could only make laws with parliament's agreement. Parliament contained some of the richest and most powerful men in the land. By the end of Elizabeth's reign there were over 500 men in parliament.

▶ William Cecil was one of Elizabeth's most important advisers.
The queen said to him:

*You shall be in my Privy Council to work hard for me and my country. You will give me the advice that you think best, even when you know that I may not agree.*

He served her faithfully all his life. She rewarded him by making him a lord.

Parliament only met when the king or queen asked it to. Its job was to agree to raise the taxes which the monarch needed, and to pass new laws. During Elizabeth's reign, some members of parliament wanted to talk about other things too. They even tried to tell Elizabeth that she should get married. She was furious.

▲ This picture shows Henry VIII opening parliament in 1523. How can you tell from the picture that there were important churchmen in parliament?

## Things to do

- Look at these statements. Which is correct? Find as much information as you can from this chapter to show why you made your choice.

'Kings and queens enjoyed themselves all the time and had no worries because they were rich.'

'Kings and queens were very powerful, but they needed advisers to help them and they could only make new laws with parliament's agreement.'

'Kings and queens had to do what parliament and their advisers told them.'

# Father and son

Henry VII and his son, Henry VIII were the first two Tudor rulers. They each faced many problems.

## How did these kings deal with their problems?

*Henry VII and Elizabeth of York*

### Think about

- Why did Henry VII choose a red and white rose as the symbol of the Tudors? The pictures of Henry and his wife Elizabeth will help you guess.

### Keeping the peace

Henry became king after defeating King Richard III in the Battle of Bosworth in 1485. This battle ended 30 years of fighting between the two families of York and Lancaster known as the Wars of the Roses. At this time nobles had their own private armies. Henry VII made sure that England became peaceful again. He passed laws to stop noblemen fighting each other. He also married Elizabeth of York. Henry was related to the Lancaster family, so by marrying Elizabeth he joined the families together and stopped the fighting.

## Defending the kingdom

Henry VIII was the son of Henry VII. When his father died he became king. He was 17 years old.

Henry VIII's father had made the monarchy rich. Henry VIII spent a lot of this money on wars. He built up a large navy. He built forts along the south coast of England in case the French invaded.

## The search for an heir

Henry wanted to have a son who could become king after him. He believed that if he did not have a son, England would be in danger. A son would stop other people from fighting to become king and destroying England's peace. It was, therefore, very important to Henry to have a wife who could give him healthy sons.

▶ This is a painting of Henry VIII.

● Which of these words describe him?

proud
confident
weak
nervous
boastful
important
frightened
determined
powerful
rich

## Henry VIII and his six wives

Henry's first wife, a Spanish princess called Catherine of Aragon, gave birth five times but only one child, Mary, survived for more than a few weeks. Henry and Catherine were married for 24 years but Henry's problem was that he needed a male heir. In 1530 he decided to divorce Catherine. He wanted to marry Anne Boleyn. The king's next problem was that the Pope would not allow divorce so Henry got divorced without permission. He then married Anne. She had a baby shortly afterwards but, to Henry's disappointment, it was a girl – Elizabeth. By 1536 Anne had still not had a son and Henry wanted to marry someone else. Anne was put on trial and beheaded. Henry married again and his third wife, Jane Seymour, gave him a son called Edward. She died shortly after the birth. Henry married another three times.

▲ Catherine of Aragon

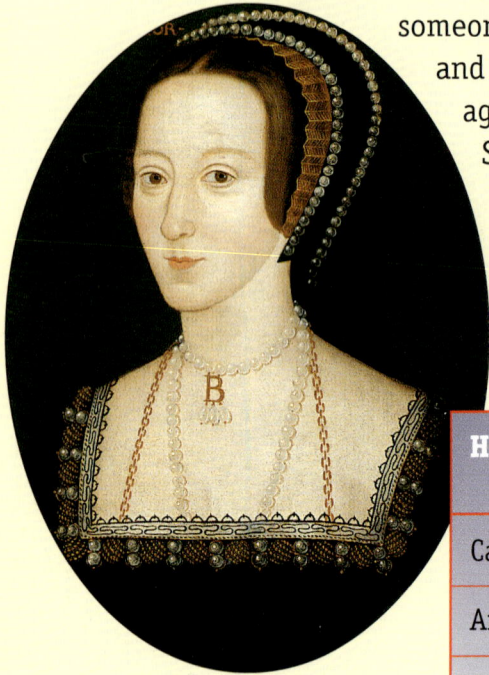

▲ Anne Boleyn

▼ This table shows what happened to Henry's wives.

| Henry's wives | When they married | How it ended |
|---|---|---|
| Catherine of Aragon | 1509 | divorced in 1533 |
| Anne Boleyn | 1533 | beheaded in 1536 |
| Jane Seymour | 1536 | died in childbirth 1537 |
| Anne of Cleves | 1540 | divorced in 1540 |
| Catherine Howard | 1540 | beheaded in 1542 |
| Catherine Parr | 1543 | Henry died before her in 1547 |

## The break with Rome

The Pope was the head of the Roman Catholic Church. He was very powerful. Most European countries were Catholic. Many people were shocked when Henry VIII disobeyed the Pope. Henry now decided to go even further. A law was passed by parliament in 1534 making Henry head of the Church of England instead of the Pope.

## Things to find

◀ This picture shows that Henry VIII took control of the Church of England.

● Find Henry VIII and the Pope. What kinds of people are trying to help the Pope?

● The man standing beside Henry became the new Archbishop of Canterbury, the most important position in the new Church of England. The artist has written his name on his sleeve. What is it?

● Who do you think made the picture: a supporter of Henry VIII or a supporter of the Pope? Explain your answer.

## Closing the monasteries

Now that Henry was in charge he could do what he liked with the Church. Henry was running out of money to pay for his soldiers and forts and he was afraid that the Spanish would soon attack. The King of Spain was angry that Henry VIII had divorced his wife, Catherine of Aragon, who was a Spanish princess. He was also angry at the way Henry had treated the Pope. Henry knew that many monasteries and abbeys were very rich. In 1536 he began to close all the monasteries. He took their lands and riches for himself.

This is Rievaulx Abbey in North Yorkshire. It was one of the monasteries closed in Henry VIII's reign.

- How can you tell from this photograph that the monastery was once very wealthy?

## A king's problem

*Who will become king when I die? I need a son.*

*The Church takes money from my country for its taxes in Rome. What does England get in return?*

*The Church is very rich. I need money to pay for my expensive court and my foreign wars.*

*I don't like the Pope telling me what to do in my country.*

*Many people complain that priests and monks are not spending enough time on their religious duties.*

- Read what Henry is saying in the picture.
  How did closing the monasteries help Henry to solve these problems?

### Things to do

- You have been reading about some of the problems which faced Henry VII and Henry VIII. You have also read about the ways in which they tried to solve these difficulties. Look at the following lists of problems and solutions. They have been jumbled up. Can you link each problem with a solution?

| Problems | Solutions |
|---|---|
| There had been fighting between the families of York and Lancaster. | Henry VIII built forts and a strong navy. |
| England had enemies in Europe. | Henry VII married Elizabeth of York. |
| A king became desperate if he had no son to become the next king. | Henry VIII closed the rich monasteries. |
| Some Tudor monarchs were short of money. | Henry VIII divorced his first wife and had his second wife beheaded. |

25

# The poor

Tudor writers often said that there were more and more poor people wandering the country, begging. They thought that many of these beggars were just lazy people who should be punished.

## Why was the number of beggars growing in Tudor times?

Historians today do not think that the beggars were all lazy people. They try to understand how changes in the country forced some men and women to become beggars. The gap between rich and poor people was getting wider. There was hardly any help for people without jobs or money. As a result, some poor people left their country village to find work. If they were unlucky and did not find work, they were forced to beg.

▼ The centre of this modern picture is a copy of 'The rich man and the poor man' which was drawn in 1569. The artist has looked carefully at the original drawing and tried to extend it, adding more details.

● Which clues in the Tudor source has the artist used to help him extend the picture?

## Rich farmers were getting richer

The population was growing. More people bought food from rich farmers.

Food prices went up. This meant more money for rich farmers.

Farms were getting bigger. Big farms made more money.

## Poor country people were getting poorer

The population was growing. There were not enough jobs in the countryside.

Food prices went up. Poor people found it hard to feed their families.

Farms were getting bigger. There were fewer small farms for poorer farmers.

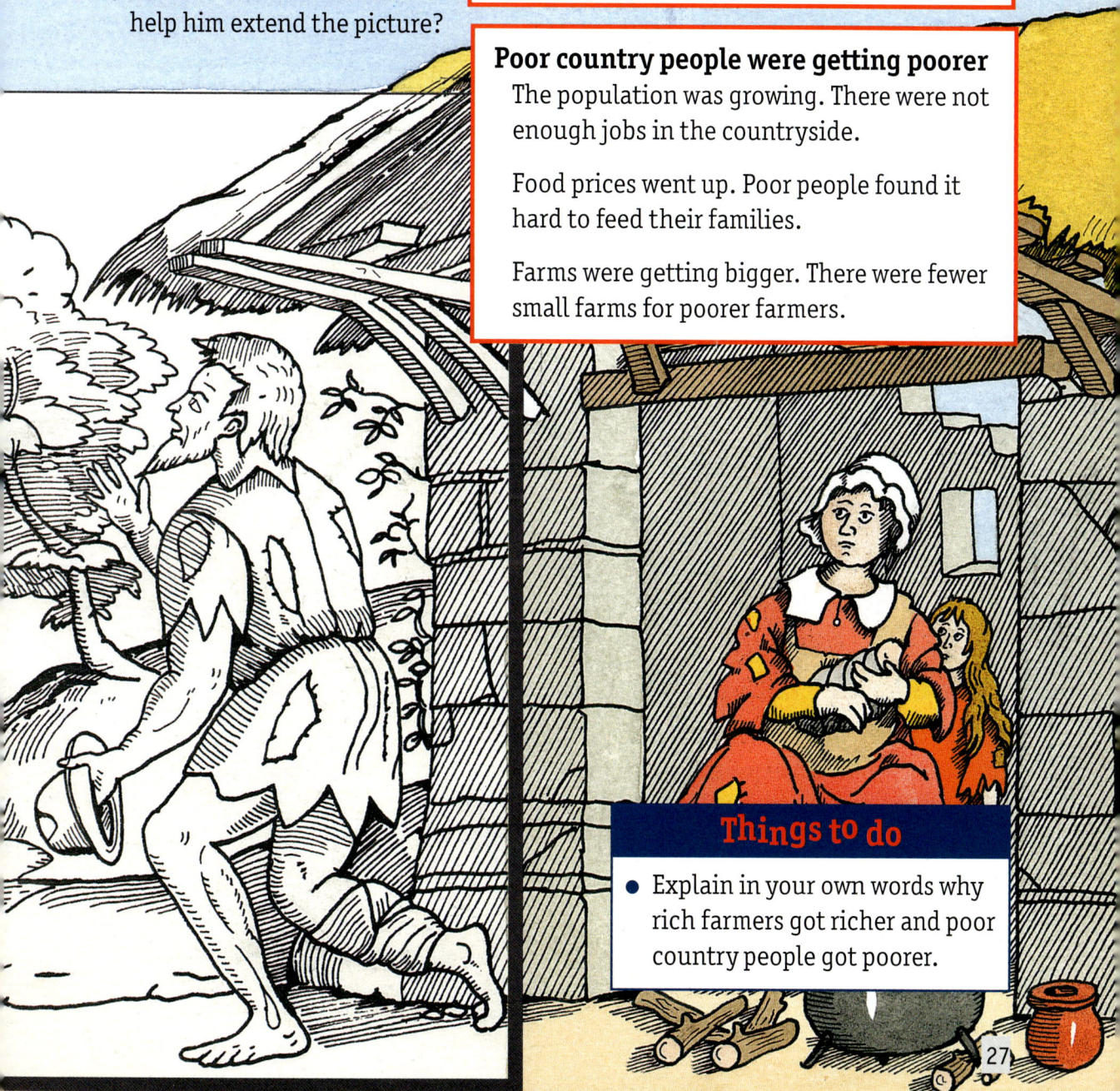

### Things to do

● Explain in your own words why rich farmers got richer and poor country people got poorer.

## Punishing the poor

Richer people were annoyed and frightened by beggars who sometimes came into town in large groups. For most of Tudor times all beggars were treated as criminals. They were whipped or had part of an ear cut off. If they were caught several times they could be hanged.

- What different types of punishments for beggars can you see in these pictures?

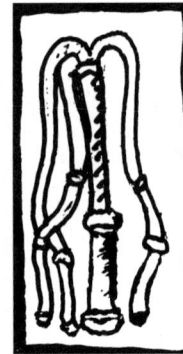

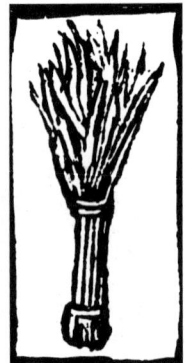

## Changing attitudes

Gradually people changed their ideas about the poor. In 1601, at the very end of the Tudor period, a new law was passed. This said that not all beggars were lazy. Rich people were told to pay a tax called the Poor Rate. This money was given to the poor who could not work because they were sick or old. Beggars who were thought to be lazy were still punished very severely.

### Think about

- Why do you think Tudor people punished beggars so harshly?

- Why would beggars join large groups before going to town?

# Crime

Crime is often in the news today. You might be surprised to know that it was also a great problem in Tudor times. Theft was by far the most common crime in the towns and cities.

## How did the Tudors punish criminals?

Some crimes were very different in Tudor times. During Elizabeth's reign people were fined if they did not go to church. In the reign of Mary Tudor some people were even burnt to death because of their religion. People believed in magic, and witches could be put to death.

▲ 'Swimming a witch'. Suspected witches were tied up and thrown into water. If they floated they were thought to be guilty.

• Tudor people had ordinary trials with judges and juries. Why do you think they sometimes used a different sort of test for witches?

# Tudor rogues

In Tudor times there were more criminals in cities, particularly in London, than in the countryside. In some cities there were special laws to control crime. In towns it was against the law to walk around the streets late at night.

▲ This picture shows a bellman of London. It was his job to ring a bell and tell people to go indoors at night.

Criminals were often known as 'rogues'. Some of them had special names. You can see two of them in this modern illustration. One is a 'cut-purse'; the other is a 'hooker'.

- What crimes are they committing?
- How does this explain their names?

In Tudor times people were often fined but jails were not used as much as they are today. If you broke the law you were more likely to be whipped or hanged. Thieves sometimes had their ears or hands cut off or were branded with a hot iron. These punishments took place in public as a way of warning other people to behave themselves.

## Rogues' language

Rogues did their best not to be caught. They had a secret language. Here are some of the words they used:

*boozing ken*  ale house

*a cony*  an easy victim

*darkmans*  night

*greenmans*  fields

*mort*  woman

*a bung*  a purse

*cove*  man

*to draw*  to pick a pocket

*lift*  rob a shop

*prig*  steal

## Things to do

- What similarities and differences are there between crime today and crime in Tudor times?

- Using as much information as you can about crime and Tudor rogues, write a conversation between two people planning a crime. Use the rogues' secret language.

# Armada

The Armada was a fleet of Spanish ships which was defeated by the English navy in a great sea battle in 1588. Ever since then, English children have been taught that the defeat of the Armada was one of the greatest moments in English history.

## Why was the defeat of the Armada so important?

Religion was very important for Tudor people and it was important in other countries too. Nearly everybody believed in God and they were frightened of disobeying Him. Most countries in Europe were Christian, but there were different kinds of Christianity. Protestants and Catholics each thought that their own type of Christianity was the right one and that God was on their side. In the 16th century, England became a Protestant country. Spain stayed Catholic.

**King Philip II of Spain**

He was a strong Catholic. He thought that God wanted him to make England a Catholic country.

## Elizabeth I of England

She was a Protestant. She was worried that Catholics wanted to replace her with a Catholic monarch.

**N**

### Key
Land under Spanish control ⬤ (yellow)
Land under English control ⬤ (red)

### Things to do

Look at all the information on these two pages.

● Can you work out one of the reasons why England and Spain became enemies.

## The story of the Armada

This is how the story of the Armada might have been told by an English courtier living at that time.

The Spanish conquered many lands in South America and found much gold and silver there. Our sailors, like Sir Francis Drake, wanted some of this wealth but the Spanish complained that they were stealing from their ships.

At the same time, our Queen feared that people wanted to kill her and to put a Catholic on the throne of England. So Queen Elizabeth ordered that Mary Queen of Scots, her Catholic cousin, should be executed.

Then King Philip of Spain sent an Armada to invade England. But the Spanish were doomed to fail against our great fleet.

The English commanders, Admiral Howard and Sir Francis Drake, ordered that some of our ships should be set on fire and allowed to drift into the Spanish fleet. The Spanish had to sail off quickly. Then a great wind blew. Sixty Spanish ships were sunk and less than half the Spanish fleet returned home. The Spanish did not attack us again.

## Things to do

- Write the story of the Spanish Armada as if you were a Spanish courtier serving King Philip of Spain. In what ways is your story different from this one?

▲ This portrait of Elizabeth was painted after the defeat of the Spanish.
  ● Find the Armada and the storm.
  ● Why do you think that Elizabeth's right hand is resting on a globe?

▶ Elizabeth had a special medal made to help people remember the victory over the Spanish. The words on the medal are 'God blew and they were scattered'.
  ● Elizabeth felt that the weather helped the English. How can you tell this from the medal?

# The royal progresses

Tudor kings and queens were often on the move. Queen Elizabeth spent a lot of time travelling around the country. She visited towns outside London and the houses of rich nobles in the countryside. This was called making a royal progress.

## Who gained from royal progresses?

Journeys were slow. The royal party often travelled less than ten miles a day. The queen rode on horseback or travelled in a litter or coach.

▼ This picture shows Elizabeth arriving in her coach at Nonesuch Palace in Surrey.

● Why do you think that so many people travelled with the queen?

A visit from the queen was a very special occasion and cost a town or a great noble a great deal of money. People were usually pleased and proud that the queen had chosen to visit them. For poorer people the progress could mean a day off work, a free show and free food and drink. For Elizabeth, it was useful to find out what was happening in the country.

When Elizabeth visited Coventry, the mayor gave her £100 in gold coins in a silver cup. Historians think that this is what the queen and the mayor said to each other:

Queen: *It is a good present. I have few such gifts.*

Mayor: *If it please Your Grace, there is a great deal more in it.*

Queen: *What is that?*

Mayor: *It is the hearts of all your loving subjects.*

Queen: *We thank you Mr Mayor, it is a great deal more indeed.*

A visitor from Spain went with Elizabeth on a progress in 1568. He wrote:

*She was greeted everywhere with great joy. She told me how beloved she was by her people. She ordered her carriage to be taken where the crowd seemed thickest.*

- Why was Queen Elizabeth so pleased with what the Mayor of Coventry said?

# The Queen visits the Earl of Hertford

Queen Elizabeth went on a royal progress in 1591. She took with her so many people that most of them had to live in tents. Local farmers and shopkeepers were very pleased because of the huge amounts of food which were bought. One morning, just for breakfast, the Queen's party ate 3 whole oxen and 140 geese.

One nobleman, the Earl of Hertford, built a special lake in the grounds of his house. The lake was used for plays, fireworks and other entertainments.

## Things to find

- Can you see where the Queen is sitting to watch the show?

- Describe what you think is happening on the lake.

▲ This picture, drawn at the time, shows the entertainment on the Earl of Hertford's lake.

*These celebrations have cost me a lot of money but it is worth it to please the queen and become one of her favourites.*

*It is good to be seen by the people in the country. I want everyone to think I am a powerful ruler.*

*There has been work for me here for weeks. I hope another lord will give me such a job again.*

## Things to do

- Different people gained from the royal visits. Look at the pictures on this page. They show: a builder, the Earl of Hertford and Queen Elizabeth. The thought bubbles show what they are thinking. Can you work out which thought bubble belongs to which person?

- Which other types of people might have gained from the royal progresses?

# Voyages of exploration

**9**

The Tudor period was a time of exploration and discovery. Countries such as Spain and Portugal were becoming rich from treasures they were taking from lands in the East and America. The English wanted their share of the wealth. English sailors began to explore the world.

## Who gained from the voyages of exploration?

In 1577 Francis Drake set off from Plymouth to sail around the world. He was the first English sailor to do this. On the journey he attacked many Spanish and Portuguese ships and stole from them. When he returned in 1580 he brought back a huge amount of treasure. Queen Elizabeth came aboard his ship and knighted him. Drake had a relative called John Hawkins. Hawkins started taking black slaves from Africa to America.

Sir Walter Raleigh sailed to North America, which was known as the New World. He landed in a place which he called Virginia in honour of the virgin queen, Queen Elizabeth. New settlements like this are called colonies. The English wanted to take land and wealth from the New World for themselves. The Spanish were already getting great wealth from their colonies in America. Walter Raleigh also brought back new plants such as tomatoes, potatoes and tobacco.

▲ Sir Francis Drake was the first English sailor to sail around the world.

In 1587 Raleigh arranged for more than 100 English people to set up another colony, called Roanoke, in North America. But when an English ship went to visit them three years later all the people had mysteriously disappeared. This picture shows the English settlers arriving in North America. Almost certainly the settlers were killed by the local people, the Native Americans. Colonies were a disaster for Native Americans as they lost control of their country.

- What does this picture tell us about the ships in Tudor times?
- What dangers might the settlers have faced?

## Think about

- Why do you think these people liked the idea of exploration:
  Queen Elizabeth, explorers
- Why do you think these people were unhappy about exploration:
  black Africans, Native Americans

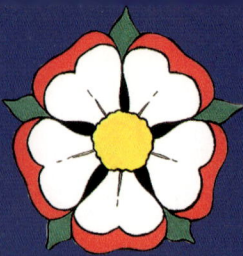

# Going to school

Growing up in Tudor times was very different from today. Not everyone went to school. The subjects children learned were not the same as those taught in school today.

## In what ways were Tudor schools different from modern schools?

Many poor children did not go to school at all. Some poor boys and girls were taught by the priest in parish schools. They learned the alphabet and how to read and write. Girls did not go to school after they were seven.

◀ This is a horn book. It was made of wood and paper covered with a thin sheet of see-through animal horn.
● What is written on the book?

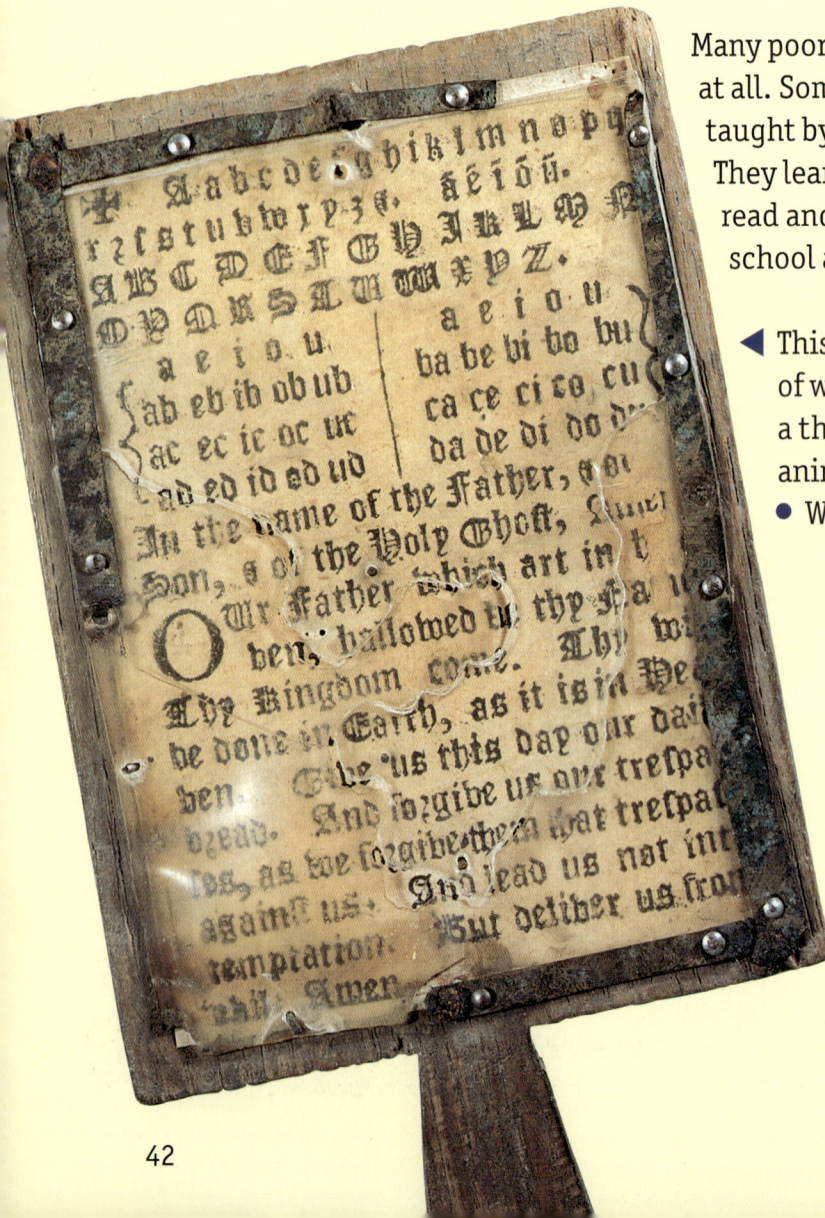

A Tudor schoolroom. ▶

## The grammar school

Most towns had a grammar school. Poor boys could not afford to go and very rich children had their own teachers at home. Boys from fairly rich families started at the grammar school at the age of about seven. The main subject was Latin and they were also taught some arithmetic and Bible stories. There was no P.E. or science. The school day lasted from about seven in the morning to four o'clock in the afternoon. Teachers were very strict and they often beat the boys with rods of birch twigs.

### Think about

- How many differences can you find between Tudor schools and schools today?
Think about:

rich and poor pupils

boys and girls

lessons

punishments

classrooms

# Shakespeare and the theatre

Plays were very popular in Tudor times. All kinds of people went to watch the actors, acrobats and puppet shows which travelled around the country. Some Tudor people thought plays were wicked. Others thought that diseases such as the plague spread more quickly in such places.

## Why was the theatre popular in Tudor times?

The Lord Mayor of London complained about theatres in 1597:

*They are common places for hiding homeless people, thieves and other idle and dangerous persons. They draw servants and apprentices away from their work and people away from church services.*

In the first half of the 16th century plays were put on in the open air in market places and inn yards. Young and old, rich and poor would come to watch popular plays which included jokes about the latest news and fashions or famous people. After about 1550 permanent theatres were built but they were very different from theatres today. They were round and had an open roof. Plays were put on in the afternoon when the weather was fine. A flag was flown to show that a play was to be performed. The theatre was a noisy place with people talking and eating. There were no curtains or scenery so the audience had to use their imaginations. The actors wore costumes and men dressed up as women because women were not allowed to act.

### Things to do

- Why did the Lord Mayor dislike the theatre?

- Imagine you are a Tudor person who likes the theatre. How would you reply to the Lord Mayor?

William Shakespeare was born in 1564. His plays are still performed today. They were very popular in Tudor times and were even acted at court for Queen Elizabeth. Some of Shakespeare's plays were funny, some were sad, but they were all written to be entertaining for all sorts of Tudor people. Sometimes the history in his plays is not accurate or even true but Shakespeare was trying to show how English kings and queens had made the country peaceful and strong. Shakespeare wrote his plays after the victory over the Armada. They show the pride that many Tudor people felt for their country.

▲ This is a model of the Rose theatre. It was based on evidence found when archaeologists excavated the site of the theatre.

# Conclusion

You have found out about many different kinds of people who lived in Tudor times. Look back through this book and think about their lives. Different kinds of people had different hopes and fears.

Monarchs would fear plots and rebellions and hope for victories over their enemies. A courtier would hope for a fine house in the country but fear falling out of favour with the monarch. A farmer would fear a poor harvest and a merchant would hope for better trade. Many of the poor would simply hope for enough to eat to stay alive.

- Make a chart showing all the different types of Tudor people you can think of. Show what each person hoped for and feared.

- Which hopes and fears are shared by different people?

- How were Tudor people's hopes and fears different from each other?

- How were Tudor people's lives different from ours today? Which of their hopes and fears were similar to our own?

- Now you can anwser this question:

# What was important to Tudor people?

# Index